TREASURE ISLAND

Robert Louis Stevenson

TECHNICAL DIRECTOR Maxwell Krohn
EDITORIAL DIRECTOR Justin Kestler
MANAGING EDITOR Ben Florman

SERIES EDITORS Boomie Aglietti, Justin Kestler
PRODUCTION Christian Lorentzen, Camille Murphy

WRITERS Brian Phillips, John Henriksen
EDITORS Karen Schrier, Matt Blanchard

This edition published by Spark Publishing

Spark Publishing
A Division of SparkNotes LLC
120 Fifth Avenue, 8th Floor
New York, NY 10011

02 03 04 05 SN 9 8 7 6 5 4 3 2 1

Please send all comments and questions or report errors to
feedback@sparknotes.com.

Library of Congress information available upon request

Printed and bound in the United States

RRD-C

ISBN 1-58663-456-9

INTRODUCTION:
STOPPING TO BUY SPARKNOTES ON A SNOWY EVENING

Whose words these are you *think* you know.
Your paper's due tomorrow, though;
We're glad to see you stopping here
To get some help before you go.

Lost your course? You'll find it here.
Face tests and essays without fear.
Between the words, good grades at stake:
Get great results throughout the year.

Once school bells caused your heart to quake
As teachers circled each mistake.
Use SparkNotes and no longer weep,
Ace every single test you take.

Yes, books are lovely, dark, and deep,
But only what you grasp you keep,
With hours to go before you sleep,
With hours to go before you sleep.

CONTENTS

NOTE: This SparkNote refers to the 1949 Random House edition of *Treasure Island*. The Random House edition divides the novel into thirty-four chapters. Most other editions divide the novel into six parts. In these editions, Part I covers Chapters I–VI of the Random House edition, Part II covers Chapters VII–XII, Part III covers Chapters XIII–XV, Part IV covers Chapters XVI–XXI, Part V covers Chapters XXII–XXVII, and Part VI covers Chapters XXVIII–XXXIV.

CONTEXT

ROBERT LOUIS (ORIGINALLY LEWIS) STEVENSON WAS born in November 1850 in Edinburgh, Scotland. His father was an engineer, and his mother was from a family of lawyers and ministers. Like many other parents of their time, the Stevensons imparted to their son the Victorian values of piety, industry, and practical success. Robert was somewhat fearful of his strict, no-nonsense father, a fact that would later be evident in the numerous antagonistic or spiritless father-son relationships depicted in his novels. Robert was a solid student, obeying his father's wishes by enrolling in Edinburgh University's engineering department with the eventual aim of joining his father's firm, which specialized in the construction of deep-sea lighthouses. Stevenson soon rebelled against this plan and reached a compromise with his father by pursuing legal studies. He frequently passed his summer vacations in France with his friends, who were mainly bohemians and artists. At the age of twenty-five, Stevenson passed the bar, but he knew he was not a lawyer at heart and never practiced. Around that time, he published his first essay, a travel piece, and his literary career began.

Stevenson's dissatisfaction with his father's practical career advice was characteristic of his broader disillusionment with the ideals of Victorian society. To Stevenson, it seemed that the entire nation considered working hard its highest duty. However, the young Stevenson frequently dreamed of escape from engineering, from Scotland, and from Victorian responsibility in general. Not surprisingly, many of his works demonstrate a sharp tension between upstanding duty and reckless abandon. Perhaps the most notable instance of this tension is *Dr. Jekyll and Mr. Hyde* (1886), in which these two opposing impulses are at war within one man, eventually tearing him apart. A later, less famous work, *The Master of Ballantrae* (1889), showcases two Scottish brothers who represent duty and recklessness, and good and evil. *Treasure Island* also features a conflict between respectful gentlemen and carefree pirates. Perhaps because of Stevenson's commitment to both duty and art, his works never clearly separate the opposing moral forces. The good and the bad are always inextricably bound to each other. As we see in *Treasure Island*, the dastardly pirate Long John Silver remarks how similar he is to the novel's upstanding young hero, Jim Hawkins.

The idea of escape was equally important in Stevenson's life and work. In 1876, on one of his visits to France, Stevenson met an American woman named Fanny Van de Grift Osbourne. At thirty-six, she was more than ten years older than he, and, furthermore, she had also been previously married and had two small children. In a most un-Victorian fashion, Stevenson fell deeply in love with Osbourne. Two years later, he followed her as she returned to California to finalize her divorce, a journey he described in *The Amateur Emigrant* (1879). Stevenson and Osbourne married in California and spent their honeymoon at an abandoned silver mine.

Stevenson got along well with Osbourne's children. It was while drawing a map with her son Lloyd that Stevenson came up with the idea of writing *Treasure Island*. The novel's focus on voyaging became even more important in Stevenson's life when his doctors advised him to seek a better climate for his health. In 1888, Stevenson and his family set sail for the South Seas, arriving in Samoa and taking up residence there in 1889. When he died in 1894, Stevenson was buried on top of Mount Vaea, an unconventional burial site that symbolizes the spirit of moral nonconformity and independent thought that he strove to convey in his works.

PLOT OVERVIEW

J IM HAWKINS IS A YOUNG boy who lives at his parents' inn, the Admiral Benbow, near Bristol, England, in the eighteenth century. An old sea captain named Billy Bones dies in the inn after being presented with a black spot, or official pirate verdict of guilt or judgment. Jim is stirred to action by the spot and its mysterious, accurate portent of Billy's death. Hastily, Jim and his mother unlock Billy's sea chest, finding a logbook and map inside. Hearing steps outside, they leave with the documents before Billy's pursuers ransack the inn.

Jim realizes that the contents he has snatched from the sea chest must be valuable, so he takes one of the documents he has found to some local acquaintances, Dr. Livesey and Squire Trelawney. Excited, they recognize it as a map for a huge treasure that the infamous pirate Captain Flint has buried on a distant island. Trelawney immediately starts planning an expedition. Naïve in his negotiations to outfit his ship, the Hispaniola, Trelawney is tricked into hiring one of Flint's former mates, Long John Silver, and many of Flint's crew. Only the captain, Smollett, is trustworthy. The ship sets sail for Treasure Island with nothing amiss, until Jim overhears Silver's plans for mutiny. Jim tells the captain about Silver and the rest of the rebellious crew.

Landing at the island, Captain Smollett devises a plan to get most of the mutineers off the ship, allowing them leisure time on shore. On a whim, Jim sneaks into the pirates' boat and goes ashore with them. Frightened of the pirates, Jim runs off alone. From a hiding place, he witnesses Silver's murder of a sailor who refuses to join the mutiny. Jim flees deeper into the heart of the island, where he encounters a half-crazed man named Ben Gunn. Ben had once served in Flint's crew but was marooned on the island years earlier.

Meanwhile, Smollett and his men have gone ashore and taken shelter in a stockade the pirates have built. Jim returns to the stockade, bringing Ben with him. Silver visits and attempts a negotiation with the captain, but the captain is wary and refuses to speak to him. The pirates attack the stockade the next day, and the captain is wounded. Eager to take action, Jim follows another whim and deserts his mates, sneaking off to hunt for Ben's handmade boat hidden in the woods.

After finding Ben's boat, Jim sails out to the anchored ship with the intention of cutting it adrift, thereby depriving the pirates of a means of escape. He cuts the rope, but he realizes his small boat has drifted near the pirates' camp and fears he will be discovered. By chance, the pirates do not spot Jim, and he floats around the island until he catches sight of the ship drifting wildly. Struggling aboard, he discovers that one of the watchmen, Israel Hands, has killed the other watchman in a drunken fit. Jim takes control of the ship, but Israel turns against him. Jim is wounded but kills Israel.

Jim returns to the stockade but finds it occupied by the pirates. Silver takes Jim hostage, telling the boy that the captain has given the pirates the treasure map, provisions, and the use of the stockade in exchange for their lives. Jim realizes, however, that Silver is having trouble managing his men, who accuse him of treachery. Silver proposes to Jim that they help each other survive by pretending Jim is a hostage. However, the men present Silver with a black spot and inform him that he has been deposed as their commander.

In a desperate attempt to gain control of his crew, Silver shows them the treasure map to appease them. Silver leads Jim and the men to the treasure site, but they are shocked to find it already excavated and the treasure removed. The men are angered and near mutiny again. At that moment Dr. Livesey, Ben Gunn, and the others fire on the pirate band, which scatters throughout the island. Jim and Silver flee, and are guided by the others to Ben's cave, where Ben has hidden the treasure, which he had discovered months before.

After spending three days carrying the loot to the ship, the men prepare to set sail for home. There is a debate about the fate of the remaining mutineers. Despite the pirates' submissive pleas, they are left marooned on the island. Silver is allowed to join the voyage, but he sneaks off the ship one night with a portion of the treasure and is never heard from again. The voyage home comes to a close. Eventually, Captain Smollet retires from the sea, and Ben becomes a lodge-keeper. Jim swears off treasure-hunting forever and suffers from nightmares about the sea and gold coins.

CHARACTER LIST

Jim Hawkins The first-person narrator of almost the entire novel. Jim is the son of an innkeeper near Bristol, England, and is probably in his early teens. He is eager and enthusiastic to go to sea and hunt for treasure. He is a modest narrator, never boasting of the remarkable courage and heroism he consistently displays. Jim is often impulsive and impetuous, but he exhibits increasing sensitivity and wisdom.

Billy Bones The old seaman who resides at Jim's parents' inn. Billy, who used to be a member of Silver's crew, is surly and rude. He hires Jim to be on the lookout for a one-legged man, thus involving the young Jim in the pirate life. Billy's sea chest and treasure map set the whole adventure in motion. His gruff refusal to pay his hotel bills symbolizes the pirates' general opposition to law, order, and civilization. His illness and his fondness for rum symbolize the weak and self-destructive aspects of the pirate lifestyle.

Black Dog A pirate and enemy of Billy. Black Dog pays an unexpected visit to Billy and threatens him. Billy attacks Black Dog, who flees but remains a herald of coming violence in the novel. Black Dog's name symbolizes both the dark and the bestial sides of piracy.

Squire Trelawney A local Bristol nobleman. Trelawney arranges the voyage to the island to find the treasure. He is associated with civic authority and social power, as well as with the comforts of civilized country life (his name suggests both "trees" and "lawn"). Trelawney's street smarts, however, are limited, as the ease with which the pirates trick him into hiring them as his crew demonstrates.

Dr. Livesey The local doctor. Dr. Livesey is wise and practical, and Jim respects but is not inspired by him. Livesey exhibits common sense and rational thought while on the island, and his idea to send Ben to spook the pirates reveals a deep understanding of human nature. He is fair-minded, magnanimously agreeing to treat the pirates with just as much care as his own wounded men. As his name suggests, Livesey represents the steady, modest virtues of everyday life rather than fantasy, dream, or adventure.

Captain Smollett The captain of the voyage to Treasure Island. Captain Smollett is savvy and is rightly suspicious of the crew Trelawney has hired. Smollett is a real professional, taking his job seriously and displaying significant skill as a negotiator. Like Livesey, Smollett is too competent and reliable to be an inspirational figure for Jim's teenage mind. Smollett believes in rules and does not like Jim's disobedience; he even tells Jim that he never wishes to sail with him again.

Long John Silver The cook on the voyage to Treasure Island. Silver is the secret ringleader of the pirate band. His physical and emotional strength is impressive. Silver is deceitful and disloyal, greedy and visceral, and does not care about human relations. Yet he is always kind toward Jim and genuinely fond of the boy. Silver is a powerful mixture of charisma and self-destructiveness, individualism and recklessness.

Ben Gunn A former pirate marooned on Treasure Island. Flint's pirate crew left Ben Gunn on the island for three years. Ben's solitude has left him somewhat deranged, and he has the appearance of a wild man. He represents a degradation of the human spirit, yet his experience has left him morally superior to the pirates. He is the only character to be reformed, as he shifts sides from the pirates to the good men, willingly helping Jim and Livesey. Ben's uncanny imitations of the dead pirate Flint's voice suggest that he is a kind of a ghost of a pirate.

Pew   An old, blind beggar and pirate. Pew presents Billy with a black spot, an ultimatum to give up the sea chest's contents to the pirate gang. Billy dies soon after Pew's visit, and Pew then dies in a carriage accident. Pew can be seen as an angel of death, foreshadowing the many pirate deaths in the novel.

Israel Hands The coxswain (a sailor who steers) on the ship. Hands is a former gunner on earlier pirate voyages. He is acting as one of two guards on the ship when the other pirates are ashore, but he gets drunk, kills the other guard, and lies in a drunken stupor while the ship drifts aimlessly. Hands symbolizes the reckless behavior of all the pirates.

Tom Redruth One of Jim's sailor companions on the ship. Tom is killed by pirate gunfire and buried with great ceremony on the island, an event that illustrates the good men's respect for the dead.

CHARACTER LIST

ANALYSIS OF MAJOR CHARACTERS

JIM HAWKINS

As the narrator of *Treasure Island* and the instigator of its most important plot twists, Jim is clearly the central character in the novel. Probably around twelve or thirteen years old, he is the quiet and obedient son of the owner of an inn near Bristol, England. As events unfold throughout the novel, Jim's character changes dramatically, showing increasing cleverness, courage, maturity, and perspective. In the first chapters, Jim is an easily frightened boy who is closely associated with his home and family. Scared by the crusty old seaman Pew, Jim runs to his mother for protection. After his father dies and he embarks on the adventure, Jim starts to think for himself and shows increasing initiative. Jim makes repeated mistakes, but he learns from them, which signals that he is maturing. He grows up quickly during this trip, starting as the cabin boy but eventually naming himself the new captain after he reclaims the ship from the pirates. Although he is courageous, Jim's impetuous individualism reminds us that he is still a youth. His tendency to act on his whims and his growing self-awareness also shows that he is caught between two worlds—between childhood and adulthood, and between the lawful, rational world and the lawless pirate world. Jim's story is therefore not merely a fanciful adventure tale but also a narrative about growing up.

Jim's narrative of his heroic acts is valuable because he records them modestly, giving us an insider view of heroism that is not very glamorous. Jim is not arrogant, but instead is humbled by his mistakes and successes. He takes full responsibility for his errors rather than finding excuses for them, and he confesses to moments of panic, indecision, and regret rather than bragging exclusively of his successes. Jim's remarkable honesty and sincerity often make the heroic or noble claims of the grown-ups—pirates and honorable citizens alike—seem like empty bluster. Jim's inclusion of both his follies and his fortunes make his narrative seem more genuine and the adventure more real.

LONG JOHN SILVER

Long John Silver is a very complex and self-contradictory character. He is cunning and mendacious, hiding his true intentions from Squire Trelawney while posing as the ship's genial cook. He is very disloyal, shifting sides so frequently that we cannot be sure of his true affiliations. He is greedy and has an almost animal nature, caring little about human relations, as we see in his cold-blooded murder of Tom Redruth. Nonetheless, Silver is without question the most vital and charismatic character in the novel. Though lacking a leg, he moves swiftly and powerfully across unsteady decks and spryly hoists himself over fences. His physical defect actually showcases his strength of character, revealing with every step his ability to overcome obstacles. Likewise, Silver's mental resolve is impressive: he is the only one of the pirates not to be spooked by Ben's imitation of the dead Flint's voice. He remains rational in the face of his men's collective superstitions, driving them forward to the treasure site. Silver's "two-hundred-year-old" parrot, which screeches dead men's words, gives the pirate an almost satanic aura. He has obvious leadership abilities, as he is able to maintain control of his ragged and surly band of mutineers to the very end of their search, through heavy losses and suspicions of treachery.

Despite Silver's formidable and frightening appearance, he is quick to inspire trust in those who meet him. Captain Smollett and Dr. Livesey both have great confidence in Silver's character at the outset of the voyage. His friendliness and politeness never seem fake, deceitful, or manipulative. Silver describes himself as a "gentleman of fortune," a term that, while clearly a euphemism for "pirate," does emphasize something genuinely gentlemanly about Silver. When Livesey requests a private chat with the hostage Jim, the other pirates protest loudly, but Silver allows it because he trusts a gentleman like Livesey. This trust on Silver's part seems noble and real. Additionally, the affection between Silver and Jim seems sincere from the very beginning. Though Jim is a mere cabin boy, Silver speaks to him fondly; toward the end of the trip, he remarks that Jim reminds him of himself when he was young and handsome. Likewise, Jim publicly calls Silver "the best man here," and his wish for Silver's happiness in the last paragraphs of the novel is sincere. Overall, Silver's behavior indicates that he is more than a mere hoodlum. There is something valuable in him for Jim's development, as the name "Silver" suggests.

DR. LIVESEY

Dr. Livesey first appears to be an ideal authority figure for the young Jim. Jim entrusts the treasure map to Livesey because Livesey is a respected, knowledgeable man. As the adventure unfolds, Livesey shows that Jim's respect is merited, proving himself competent, clever, fair, and loyal. Livesey devises the brilliant plan of stalling the pirate brigade by sending Ben Gunn to give spooky imitations of their dead leader, Flint. He also comes up with the ruse of sending the pirates on the wild-goose chase to find the treasure. Livesey is not afraid of action and bravely fires on the pirates at the treasure site. He is noble in his willingness to provide medical attention to the wounded pirates, his enemies. He speaks tenderly to them and seems genuinely to care for their health. More so than the gruff Captain Smollett or the naïve Squire Trelawney, Livesey represents the best of the civilized world of men.

Despite his credentials and valuable achievements in the tale, however, Livesey is simply not charismatic. He does what is reasonable, practical, and ethical, but never acts impetuously or spontaneously, as the pirates and Jim do. Livesey thinks up ingenious plans, but only puts them into practice if they are safe and efficient. He gives the pirates the treasure map only when he knows it is useless. On the whole, Livesey never risks anything, and therefore Jim, as we do, sees him as good but not grand, decent but not inspirational. It is significant that while Jim gives a sentimental farewell to the memory of Silver at the end of his narrative, he omits mention of Livesey, despite Livesey's importance in the adventure. Jim does not have an emotional connection to Livesey, and, by extension, does not have an emotional connection to the decent, civilized world Livesey represents. Jim does not fit completely into Silver's world, but he does not fit completely into Livesey's steady, practical world either.

CHARACTER ANALYSIS

THEMES, MOTIFS & SYMBOLS

THEMES

Themes are the fundamental and often universal ideas explored in a literary work.

THE SEARCH FOR HEROIC ROLE MODELS

Treasure Island is an adventure tale, but it is also the story of one boy's coming of age. At the outset of the novel, Jim is a timid child, but by the end he has matured incredibly. He has outwitted pirates, taken over a ship, and saved innumerable lives. Jim has become an adult in character if not in age. Like any maturing boy, Jim must try out various male role models. Jim's father does not appear to be a significant role model: he passes away early in the novel, and even before that he does not seem to have much effect on Jim's inner life. In fact, Jim scarcely mentions his father in his narrative.

Alternatively, we might expect a local authority figure to act as role model for Jim. Dr. Livesey, for example, has high social status in the community and represents the civilized, rational world. When Jim finds the map, he immediately thinks of Livesey when wondering what he should do with it. It therefore initially seems that Jim looks up to Livesey as a role model. Squire Trelawney, like the doctor, is another symbol of worldly authority. However, while both men are upstanding citizens, they do not captivate Jim's mind or inspire him. They are simply too staid and predictably upstanding.

When the pirates appear, however, Jim begins to pay close attention to their actions, attitudes, and appearance. He describes Silver with an intensity and attention to detail that he does not show for any other character. Soon, Jim is imitating some aspects of Silver's behavior. He acts impulsively and bravely when he sneaks into the pirates' boat in Chapter XIII. He even deserts his own captain in Chapter XXII, effectively enacting his own mutiny. He sails a pirate's boat out to the anchored ship, kills the pirate Israel Hands, and names himself the new captain of the ship. The pirate side of Jim is so apparent that Silver himself remarks that

Jim reminds him of what he was like as a boy, hinting that Jim
could grow up to be like Silver.

At the end of the novel, the pirates' influence on Jim's development is clear, and not necessarily detrimental. Jim displays more
courage, charisma, and independence than the captain, squire, or
doctor. Just as he has not mentioned his father, he does not mention
these men at the close of his narrative, an omission that suggests that
they have not been important to his development. Instead, Jim pays
a touching tribute to Silver and wishes the pirate well. Indeed, Silver
has been more instrumental than anyone else in shaping Jim's identity, hopes, and dreams.

THE FUTILITY OF DESIRE

Treasure Island explores the satisfaction of desires, and, indeed, the
motivation of all the characters is greed: everyone wants the treasure. By the end of the adventure, Jim and the captain's crew have
sated their greed, having won the treasure. Stevenson vividly
describes how the men haul the gold bars to the ship, as if to under-
score the final satisfying achievement. But Stevenson also casts
doubt on the possibility of ultimate satisfaction. For the pirates,
desire proves futile and goals unattainable, as the treasure map leads
them to an empty hole. The empty hole becomes a symbol for the
futility of the treasure hunt and for the loss of one's soul in searching
for the treasure. When the pirates dig in the ground, it is as if they are
digging their own grave. Their greed and irrationality lead only to
death, loss, and dissatisfaction.

Similarly, though Ben has possessed the treasure for three
months, he is half mad and living in a cave. Such treasure is useless
to him if he is alone on an island. Without the structure and rules of
a society that places monetary value on gold, the treasure is worth-
less. Likewise, we see that Jim himself is not satisfied by the gold. He
does not mention its value and focuses instead on the coins' nationality and their design. He does not refer to his share of the windfall
or to what happens to the treasure when he gets back home. The gold
coins elicit nightmares, not dreams of his riches. Jim displays no
desire to return for the remaining silver treasure left behind. Unlike
other literary adventurers such as Huckleberry Finn in Mark Twain's
The Adventures of Huckleberry Finn or Odysseus in Homer's *Odys-
sey*, Jim does not want to travel or treasure-hunt endlessly. He has
learned that the desires associated with such lifestyles are futile—he
will never attain a good life through greed and bloodshed.

TREASURE ISLAND ❧ 15

THE LACK OF ADVENTURE IN THE MODERN AGE

Stevenson frames his tale of piracy with a number of devices that emphasize the end of the story. He suggests that the tale belongs firmly to the past rather than to the present. Stevenson's decision to set the story in the eighteenth century underscores the fact that the pirate life is outmoded. Stevenson also has Jim begin his narrative in the form of a retrospective chronicle that begins after the adventure is already over. We know from the first sentence that Jim, Squire Trelawney, Smollett, and Livesey have survived as victors. This knowledge lends a tone of gloom to the pirates' first appearance, as we know they are doomed. The pirates die out rapidly over the course of the novel and are continually associated with death, disease, and disappearance. Indeed, the pirate's skeleton found near the treasure site symbolizes the pirates' impending doom.

Stevenson, however, does not glorify the death of piracy and the eradication of criminals. With Jim's final sad farewell to the memory of Silver, in which he says that he will go on no more adventures, Stevenson creates a sort of elegy to the pirate life. Stevenson does not mourn its loss, but he makes us wonder whether the world is better off without the pirates' charisma, charm, and spirit. He challenges the Victorian idea that captains, doctors, and other responsible professional men are the natural leaders of society. Stevenson was critical of stodgy Victorian professionalism throughout his life, and his somewhat romantic portrait of vanished pirates forms a sad tribute to what he feels is missing from the modern world.

MOTIFS

Motifs are recurring structures, contrasts, or literary devices that can help to develop and inform the text's major themes.

SOLITUDE

Despite Jim's solidarity with Smollett's crew, teamwork is not a dominant motif in *Treasure Island*. Instead, Stevenson emphasizes Jim's recurring moments of solitude. Though Jim does spend time with his family at the beginning of the novel and is later frequently in the company of the captain's men and the pirates' band, these intervals are punctuated by far more crucial moments during which Jim is alone. For instance, Jim is alone when he meets Pew, the pirate who delivers the black spot that sets the story in motion. He is alone in the apple barrel when he overhears the critical information about the mutiny that enables him to save Smollett. He is alone when he meets Ben Gunn in the woods and learns the directions to the treasure. Jim is also alone when he sails in the coracle to cut the ship adrift, depriving the pirates of their means of escape. Throughout the novel, Jim's instances of solitude are associated with self-reliance and show his maturity. This solitude may also have a downside, however. Jim's decision to function independently, rather than as part of a larger team, may be what prompts Smollett to tell him that they will never voyage together again. Jim may be too individualistic to make a good rank-and-file sailor.

ANIMALS

Though many works of children's literature link animals to childhood, in *Treasure Island* animals are associated not with Jim but with the pirates. Jim does not have a pet in the novel, but Long John Silver has his eerie parrot named Cap'n Flint. The parrot does not affirm Silver's humanity, but rather emphasizes the pirates' inhumanity, as the bird is witness to two centuries of heinous pirate crimes. Cap'n Flint's raucous screeching of other men's words echoes the pirates' constant singing about their greed, violence, and selfishness. The parrot's incessant mockery suggests that the pirates are better at making noise than producing intelligent statements.

The pirates resemble other animals as well. As they climb over the stockade fence in Chapter XXI, Stevenson compares them to monkeys. When Jim first sees the ex-pirate Ben Gunn in Chapter XV, he likens him to a "creature ... like a deer." Later, when Jim faces down his captors in Chapter XXVIII, they all stare at him "like as many sheep," suggesting that they are all faceless, submissive members of a herd. Notably, Stevenson never likens the captain's group to any animals, suggesting that the captain's men are decent human beings while the pirates are subhuman creatures.

THE COLOR BLACK

Stevenson also repeatedly associates the color black with the pirates. The pirate flag, the Jolly Roger, is black, in sharp contrast with the colorful British flag, the Union Jack. The pirates also give out black spots, verdicts delivered to their victims. Significantly, the pirate who discovers Billy in hiding is named Black Dog. Likewise, the pirate Pew, in his blindness, lives in a state of unending blackness. When Jim creeps among the sleeping pirates, he proceeds "where the darkness was thickest," an image that likens the pirates to chunks of blackness. Many of Jim's most frightening encounters with the pirates, such as his examination of the dead Billy, his drifting near the pirate camp on the island, and his accidental entry among the sleeping pirates in the stockade, occur in the black of the night. Certainly, as the color of funerals and mourning, black is associated with death, and the pirates leave a wake of death wherever they travel. Black is also the color of absence, the total lack of light, enlightenment, and illumination. The pirates' lack of light contrasts with the shining, glimmering gold for which they search— and which they wrongly imagine will brighten their dark lives.

SYMBOLS

Symbols are objects, characters, figures, or colors used to represent abstract ideas or concepts.

THE CORACLE
Jim discovers the coracle—the small boat that Ben Gunn has constructed out of wood and goatskin—at the end of Chapter XXII. In the chapters that follow, Jim uses the coracle to sail out to the Hispaniola, cut it adrift, ruin the pirates' chances of escape, and climb aboard to kill Israel Hands. The irony of a small boy using a small boat to overpower a large man in a large ship points to a David-and-Goliath symbolism in Jim's adventure. Indeed, Jim ultimately proves a victorious underdog.

However, the coracle, which belongs to a former pirate, also symbolizes Jim's desertion of Captain Smollett. In leaving his superior to go hunt for the boat, Jim becomes a bit like a pirate himself. His heroism is not unequivocally good in a moral sense, which may be why the captain does not wish Jim to accompany him on any more voyages. Despite Jim's disloyalty, his adventurous spirit leads him eventually to save many lives and stop the pirates from escaping. The coracle therefore also represents the boy's moral ambiguity and his pirate apprenticeship.

THE TREASURE MAP
Though the treasure map appears in the novel's first chapter, when Jim and his mother ransack Billy Bones's sea chest, it retains its fascinating and mysterious aura nearly to the end of the novel. The map functions as a sort of magic talisman that draws people into the adventure story. Jim's possession of the map transforms him from

an ordinary innkeeper's son to a sailor and a hero, and changes the stodgy squire and doctor into freewheeling maritime adventurers.

In addition to symbolizing adventure, however, the map also symbolizes desire—and the vanity of desire. Everyone wants the map and seems willing to go to unbelievable ends to attain it. Ironically, however, Stevenson ultimately shows us that the map has been useless throughout the whole novel, as Ben Gunn has already excavated the treasure and moved it elsewhere. The map directs Silver, its possessor, not to a final happiness but to a significant letdown: the empty hole where the treasure should be. In this sense, the map symbolizes the futility of hunting for material satisfaction.

RUM

Rum reappears throughout the novel as a powerful symbol of the pirates' recklessness, violence, and uncontrolled behavior. In Stevenson's time, people considered rum a crude form of alcohol, the opposite of the refined and elegant wine that the captain's men occasionally drink. The pirates do not engage in light social drinking—when they indulge in rum, their drunkenness is destructive, as reflected in the pirate song lyric about the "dead man's chest." The first sailor to drink himself to death is Billy, who keeps drinking though Livesey warns him it will kill him. Later, Mr. Arrow, the first mate aboard the Hispaniola, is constantly tipsy until he falls overboard, presumably to his death. When Jim climbs on board the ship, he finds that in their rum-induced drunkenness the two watchmen have lost control of the ship and that one of them has killed the other. Jim is able to defeat his adult attacker largely because Jim is sober and Israel Hands is drunk. Rum therefore symbolizes an inability to control or manage what is one's own: one's property, one's mission, and one's very self.

SUMMARY & ANALYSIS

CHAPTERS I–III

SUMMARY: CHAPTER I

> *Fifteen men on the dead man's chest—*
> *Yo-ho-ho, and a bottle of rum!*
> *Drink and the devil had done for the rest—*
> *Yo-ho-ho, and a bottle of rum!*
> (See QUOTATIONS, p. 47)

At the urging of Squire Trelawney, Dr. Livesey, and others, a boy named Jim Hawkins records his story about Treasure Island. He omits the island's exact location, as a portion of its treasure still remains buried there. Jim begins the story by recounting his first meeting with a ragged but imposing old seaman who shows up at the Admiral Benbow, the inn Jim's father owns.

The old sailor throws down a few gold coins and moves in, staying at the inn for far longer than his payment covers. He hires Jim to stay on the lookout for a one-legged sailor whom he apparently fears. He terrorizes the others in the inn with his coarse sailor's songs and heavy drinking. Livesy cautions the sailor about the dangers of drinking, but these warnings enrage the seaman, who threatens Livesey with a knife. Livesey subdues the man with his calm authority.

> *[I]f you keep on drinking rum, the world will soon be*
> *quit of a very dirty scoundrel!*
> (See QUOTATIONS, p. 48)

SUMMARY: CHAPTER II

On a cold January morning soon after, a tall pale man who is missing two fingers enters the inn. The man asks Jim if he has seen his mate Bill, or Billy Bones, as he is generally called, who is recognizable by a scar on one cheek. Jim knows the stranger is referring to the old seaman who is staying at the inn, and he tells the stranger that Bill will be back soon. Bill returns, and he gasps when he recognizes his former shipmate, whom he addresses as Black Dog. The two launch into a violent conversation that Jim cannot hear. The conversation ends as Billy Bones attempts to kill Black Dog with his sword, but he is cut short, as he suddenly succumbs to a stroke. Livesey cares for Billy in the inn and warns him to stay away from rum, which in his ill health would be lethal for him.

SUMMARY: CHAPTER III

Jim attends to the ailing Billy, who begs him for a swig of rum in return for some money. Jim is offended, saying he wants only what Billy owes his father for rent. But he gives Billy one glass of rum. Energized by the alcohol, Billy says he must quickly get moving to outsmart his pursuers. He explains to Jim that the former crew of the ship he sailed on, under the now-dead Captain Flint, wants his sea chest. That night Jim's father, who has also been ill, dies.

Returning from his father's funeral, Jim encounters a sinister blind man who asks to be taken to Billy. Billy appears sickened to see the blind man, who hands him a black spot, which Jim has learned represents an official secret pirate summons. Reading the black spot, Billy enigmatically cries out that he has only six hours left. He springs into to action, but falls down, stricken with a fatal stroke. Jim is worried and calls for his mother.

ANALYSIS: CHAPTERS I–III

Stevenson begins his adventure tale with the unusual device of a young male narrator, giving the narrative an innocent and straightforward tone. This tone eases our entry into the dark criminal underworld of pirates and murderers. Since most readers are typically unfamiliar with such shady figures, Jim's wide-eyed awe of them mirrors our own perspective. Jim is meek and fearful of the pirates' drunken, swaggering, coarse language and tendency toward violence. When he calls out for his mother at the end of Chapter III, we are reminded that he is a scared little boy, and indeed a world apart from the sailors. Stevenson's emphasis on Jim's childishness in these early chapters highlights the degree to which Jim matures throughout the novel. Later, Jim is no longer cowed by the grizzly seamen and holds his own against them. Here at the beginning, however, the contrast between the narrator's innocence and the characters' worldly experience helps set the stage for the rite of passage into adulthood that Jim later undergoes.

The device of the boy narrator also allows Stevenson to emphasize the fascinating, enthralling allure of the pirates. Jim is clearly entranced by these ragged, powerful, and outlandish men, much more so than by his own father, who is ordinary and unexciting by comparison. Jim hardly mentions his parents, even after his father's death. Though the narrative hints that the pirates are morally bad, Jim admires them all the same. As Stevenson surely understood, many readers can relate to the romanticizing of the pirate life, and the fantasy of becoming a pirate may inspire our own wide-eyed fantasies. Indeed, Stevenson encourages us to fantasize and use our imaginations by having the young Jim thrillingly refer to the treasure that still lies buried on the island. The idea of this treasure prompts us to create our own daydreams of finding it. Sharing Jim's fantasies allows us to become greater participants in *Treasure Island*, and enables us to relate to Jim even more strongly.

In these first chapters, Stevenson begins to show the vast difference between the upstanding world of doctors, housewives, and small business owners, and the sinister world of pirates. Though the conflict between these two sides does not reach its peak until a battle between the good and the bad much later in *Treasure Island*, the roots of this conflict are here in these opening chapters. Billy Bones bullies Jim's parents enough to frighten them out of collecting the rent he owes them, suggesting that the world of law and order is powerless again a pirate's brute force and charisma. Even the blind man, whom we later learn is named Pew, becomes a figure of terror, immense in his criminal glamour. However, in the scene in which Livesey coolly rebuffs Billy's knifepoint threats, we sense that the sides of crime and justice may be evenly matched, and that the balance between them is very delicate. This scene is an early exploration of one of Stevenson's central ideas in the novel—the frequent opposition between social lawfulness and personal charisma.

CHAPTERS IV–VI

SUMMARY: CHAPTER IV

Jim tells his mother about the pirates' plot to take Billy's sea chest, and he flees with her to the neighboring village to seek help. Terrified by the name of old Flint, none of the villagers is willing to go to the inn to offer assistance. Armed with a gun, Jim returns with his mother to the inn. He searches through the dead Billy's clothing to find the key to the treasure chest. Finding the key around Billy's neck, Jim and his mother open the chest and find gold hidden at the bottom, a portion of which Jim's mother claims as her due. They hear running footsteps in the street outside. Jim takes some papers wrapped in an oilcloth that he has found in the sea chest and then flees the inn with his mother. Weakened by fear, his mother faints outside. Jim succeeds in dragging her under a bridge, out of sight but within earshot of the inn.

SUMMARY: CHAPTER V

Terrified but curious, Jim looks out from his hiding place. He sees seven or eight men running toward the inn, among them the blind man who had visited before. The eight men are surprised to find the inn door open and Billy dead. They are concerned about the chest and seem disappointed that it contains only Billy's money: clearly they are more interested in something else that belonged to Flint. The blind man, whom the others address as Pew, orders the men to scatter and find the fugitives. He reminds them that they could be as rich as kings if they find the missing object.

Enraged, Pew starts screaming at his men, and they all begin to quarrel violently. Hearing a pistol shot, however, the men panic and flee, leaving the blind Pew alone on the road. Pew is accidentally run down and killed by men on horseback who have come to investigate. Returning home, Jim finds the inn ruined. He realizes that the oilcloth-wrapped papers in his pocket may be what the pirates sought, but he is reluctant to hand them over to the officer, Dance, who tries to take charge of the situation. Jim says he would prefer to show the papers to Dr. Livesey, and he sets off with Dance's party for Livesey's house.

SUMMARY: CHAPTER VI

Jim, Dance, and the others arrive at Dr. Livesey's darkened house to learn that he is dining at the home of Squire Trelawney, a local nobleman. The group heads to Trelawney's residence, where they find the two men in the library. Livesey examines the oilskin packet that Jim has recovered. Trelawney claims that the pirate Flint is more bloodthirsty than Blackbeard and has accumulated a huge fortune. They open the book wrapped in the oilskin and find that it is a log of all the places where Flint acquired loot, and of the sums of gold that he obtained in each place. The packet also includes a map of the island where the whole treasure now lies buried, with longitude and latitude detailed. Trelawney and Livesey are filled with glee, and start making plans to sail to the island themselves, bringing Jim along as cabin boy. Everyone present swears to secrecy.

ANALYSIS: CHAPTERS IV–VI

In this section, Jim is already beginning to develop as a character and as a hero. Whereas in the first chapters he wants to run to his mother out of fear, here it is his mother who faints in terror and Jim who drags her to a safe hiding place. Now the male head of the household, Jim shows courage and quick-wittedness. When examining the contents of the sea chest, Jim's mother seeks to take only the money Billy owes her, whereas Jim has the foresight to take the valuable oilskin packet containing the map of Treasure Island. Facing Billy's dead body, Jim's mother sobs and complains that she could never touch it, while Jim tears open the corpse's shirt and finds the key to the chest. Furthermore, after Pew's death and the arrival of the town officers on the scene, Jim bravely rejects officer Dance's request for the map. Jim voices his preference to take the map to Livesey instead, the event that sets the whole adventure in motion. It is hard to imagine that the meek little boy of Chapter I would have taken any of these bold actions; indeed, Jim is growing up quickly.

The aura of mystery and excitement surrounding the pirates grows in these chapters. Jim's vision of Pew suggests that these pirates are superhuman, as Pew appears much more powerful than one would expect a blind beggar to be. Like many of the other pirates, Pew is physically flawed. He lacks sight, just as Billy lacks overall health and Long John Silver, as we soon see, lacks a leg. Yet these pirates' inner strength appears to compensate for their physical flaws. This inner power and charisma captivates the young Jim, even as it strikes fear into the villagers. None of the good men has any force of personality or charisma comparable to that of the pirates. Though Trelawney applauds Dance for killing Pew, whom he compares to a cockroach, it is Pew who acts heroically in the streets while Trelawney dines comfortably in his library. In this way, Stevenson subtly sketches the buccaneers as mysteriously attractive, in spite of their immoral and crude outward behavior. He likewise makes it difficult for us to conclude that men like Trelawney are unambiguously superior to the pirates.

Somewhat surprisingly, perhaps, Livesey and Trelawney, the respectable members of local society, become boyishly excited and

"filled ... with delight" upon seeing Flint's map. Rather than turn
the documents over to the authorities and turn their backs on the
dark underworld of piracy and thievery, they are thrilled at the
idea of becoming pirate adventurers themselves. The upstanding
Trelawney immediately launches into a schoolboy's fantasy of
finding "favorable winds, a quick passage, and not the least difficulty in finding the spot, and money to eat—to roll in—to play
duck and drake with ever after." The image the pirates have left in
Trelawney's mind is not one of crime and murder, but one of fun,
games, and riches. The readiness of these responsible and professional grown men to become adventurous boys again is part of a
theme central to this novel: Stevenson implies that there is a little
pirate in everyone, old or young, nobleman or beggar. In this sense,
Jim begins to emerge not as the token boy in the novel, but as rep-
resentative of all the characters, no matter what their age or position in life.

Chapters VII–XII

Summary: Chapter VII

After a frustrating delay in preparations for the journey to Treasure
Island, Jim is pleased to hear that Dr. Livesey has received a letter
from Squire Trelawney describing the ship and crew that he has
obtained. The ship has been procured through one of Trelawney's
acquaintances in Bristol, a man who seems all too ready to help him
and has a poor reputation in the city.

The ship is called the Hispaniola. Trelawney relates that he had
some trouble finding a crew for the voyage until he had the good fortune to meet up with an old one- legged sailor named Long John Silver. Silver tells Trelawney that he misses the sea and wishes to set sail
again as the ship's cook. Trelawney hires him, and Silver helps
arrange the rest of the crew as well.

After a sad farewell with his mother, Jim sets out the next morning for Bristol, accompanied by Tom Redruth, another man who
will be on the ship's crew. At the inn in Bristol, they meet up with
Trelawney, newly clothed in a sea officer's outfit. Trelawney informs
them that they will sail the next day.

SUMMARY: CHAPTER VIII

*I don't put much faith in your discoveries . . . but I
will say this, John Silver suits me.*

(See QUOTATIONS, p. 49)

Trelawney gives Jim a note to pass on to Long John Silver at the
Spy-glass, a tavern in the town. Jim sets off happily to find the
sailor. Silver is more clean-cut than Jim expects, but Jim recognizes
him and introduces himself. Just then, another customer in the bar
suddenly gets up to leave, attracting Jim's attention. Jim recognizes
the man as Black Dog and informs Silver. Jim is pleased to learn
that Silver shares his negative view of Black Dog and Pew. Silver
wins over Jim's trust, and they stroll by the docks as Silver tells Jim
about ships and sea life. Silver is introduced to Dr. Livesey and
treats him with respect. Likewise, Livesey is quite pleased to have
Silver as the ship's new cook.

SUMMARY: CHAPTER IX

While boarding the ship, Jim, Silver, and the others meet Mr.
Arrow, the first mate, with whom Trelawney gets along well. There
is some animosity, however, between Trelawney and the captain,
whose name is Smollett. Smollett is very opinionated, and speaks
openly about his dislike of most of the crew and about the fact that
he has a bad feeling about the voyage. Smollett also adds that there
has been too much blabbing about the map and the treasure, though
Trelawney protests that he has told no one. After the captain leaves,
Livesey asserts that he trusts Silver and Smollett completely.

SUMMARY: CHAPTER X

The voyage begins on an ominous note, as the first mate, Mr. Arrow,
turns out to be a hopeless drunk who is useless on board. He disappears mysteriously one night, leading the others to presume that he
fell overboard in his drunkenness. The boatswain, Job Anderson,
replaces Arrow. Jim continues to be entranced by Silver, impressed
by his swift one-legged maneuverings around the deck. Jim is also
fascinated by Silver's two-hundred-year-old parrot, which is named
Cap'n Flint, after the famed buccaneer. Relations between
Trelawney and Smollett are still somewhat strained, but the voyage
proceeds normally. One evening, Jim gets hungry for an apple and
climbs into an apple barrel on board, where, unsuspected, he overhears an important conversation.

Summary: Chapter XI

Hiding in the apple barrel, Jim overhears Long John Silver telling several other crewmembers about some of his adventures with old Flint. Silver mentions that he has nearly three thousand pounds safely hidden away in the bank, gained from his exploits with the other "gentlemen of fortune," which Jim correctly guesses is just another word for pirates. Jim learns that most of old Flint's former crewmembers are on board the ship now, posing as ordinary crew but plotting to take the treasure for themselves. Silver mentions that some of the other crewmembers have joined the conspirators, though others have refused. Jim watches the pirates partake of a secret stash of rum. As the men drink, the cry of "Land ho!" is heard from on deck.

Summary: Chapter XII

With the island visible before them, Smollett and his crew discuss the best place to drop anchor. Smollett consults a map of the island, and Jim notices that it is an exact copy of the treasure map he saw before, but without the "X" marking the treasure's hiding place. Silver knows the island well, and offers advice, enthusiastically telling Jim how much he enjoys the island. Smollett congratulates the crew on a job well done, and then meets with Trelawney below deck. Later, Jim goes below deck and warns Smollett and Trelawney about Silver's criminal intentions, telling them what he overheard while hiding in the apple barrel. Trelawney immediately admits that he has been a fool in hiring the crew and trusting Silver. Smollett urges everyone to stay vigilant.

Analysis: Chapters VII–XII

As the journey to Treasure Island unfolds, and the familiar landscape of England gives way to the contours of the unknown island, boundaries and roles become more ambiguous. The crew that earlier seems docile and friendly now seems resentful and sour, even hostile. The first mate, Mr. Arrow, whom Trelawney initially likes very much, is revealed to be a useless drunkard after only a few days at sea. Likewise, Silver is not the staunch supporter of the captain that he initially appears to be. The conversation Jim overhears shows that Silver and a majority of the ship's crew are thoroughly disloyal. Even Jim's role on the ship turns out to be very different than originally planned, as he quickly breaks out of the limited role of a mere cabin boy. Livesey calls Jim the most useful person on the ship, as he is perceptive and not suspected by the conspirators. As we see the once-loyal crew shift to the side of the mutineers and the cabin boy become a hero, we see that human character is indeed quite malleable.

These changing roles on the ship challenge established ideas about social hierarchy and authority, and give precedence to a non-traditional set of values. The old order and power structure gives way to a new one that is based on strength and charisma. Before the voyage begins, Squire Trelawney is clearly in the position of greatest control and resents the fact that Captain Smollett does not show him what he considers due respect. Mr. Arrow, as first mate, occupies a position only slightly subordinate to Trelawney. Jim, as the cabin boy, is on the lowest rung of the power ladder, and Silver, as the ship's cook, also seems to be a minor figure. Immediately after the ship sets sail, however, Silver wins Jim's respect with his nimble one-legged movement around the deck, while the authority of the boozy first mate Mr. Arrow quickly collapses. When Trelawney finally admits that he was a fool to trust the crew, the old system of power relationships and authority finally unravels. Now, Stevenson suggests, a new society must develop—not according to the inherited titles and wealth that have given power to men like Trelawney, but according to the very different principles of cleverness, fortitude, and perceptiveness.

Stevenson develops the character of Long John Silver intensely in these chapters, and shows him to be a very complex man. On the one hand, Silver's motivation for seeking the treasure is no different from what motivates Trelawney and Livesey: greed and a love for the pirate life. Indeed, Silver is merely after money in the bank and a life of leisure ahead—the kind of life Trelawney already enjoys. Though Silver may be looking for fortune the wrong way, his goal of having a good life for himself is not in itself criminal. On the other hand, however, Silver displays an ability to mask his true feelings and motives to an almost devilish degree, raising a cheer for the captain whom he secretly hates, fooling everyone with his fake applause. Though Jim knows Silver is disappointed to see the map with no "X" on it, Silver shows no signs of this disappointment. He is a master of duplicity in a way that approaches evil. Indeed, Silver himself refers to this evil side, remarking in Chapter X about all the "wickedness" his parrot has seen.

CHAPTERS XIII–XV

SUMMARY: CHAPTER XIII

Having approached the island in sweltering weather, the crew is irritable and discontent. Dr. Livesey warns the men that they may be at risk of contracting tropical diseases on the island. Silver, with his knowledge of the island's geography, advises Captain Smollett of a good place to drop anchor. Smollett does not reveal what he knows about the planned mutiny. After consulting with Squire Trelawney, he decides to allow the crew to go ashore for diversion, which allows the honest men to reclaim control of the ship.

Smollett takes Tom Redruth and several other honest sailors into his confidence and gives them weapons. Silver leads the pirates ashore, believing that they will be able to recover the treasure immediately. Jim, deciding that his assistance is not needed on board, hides in one of the pirates' boats and goes ashore with them. However, Silver catches sight of Jim, who begins to regret his decision. Reaching the shore before the others, Jim quickly scrambles away from them.

SUMMARY: CHAPTER XIV

As Jim surveys the island, he is startled to hear voices nearby. He creeps closer and finds Silver addressing one of the sailors named Tom, trying to persuade him to join the mutineers. Silver makes it clear that Tom's life is riding on his decision, but Tom declines politely but firmly. They suddenly hear a piercing scream from far away, and Tom is greatly alarmed. Silver says coldly that the scream must be from Alan, another honest sailor who has refused to join the pirates.

Tom tells Silver that Silver is his friend no more and starts to walk away. Silver flings his crutch at Tom's back, knocking him down, and then walks over and kills him with his knife. Jim is terrified, realizing that he has no way to get back to the ship without being spotted and killed by Silver and his gang. Jim starts to run deeper into the island.

SUMMARY: CHAPTER XV

Fleeing the pirates, Jim sees a human figure in the woods, and he fears that it is a cannibal. Suddenly remembering he is armed, Jim gains courage and walks briskly toward the man, who is hiding behind a tree. Jim asks the man his name, and the man replies that his name is Ben Gunn and that he has been on the island for three years. Jim asks Ben if he was shipwrecked, and Ben answers that he was marooned. Ben speaks in a deranged manner, making many religious allusions. Jim suspects that Ben may be mad.

When Ben asks if the ship moored on the shore is Flint's, Jim realizes the wild man may have useful information. Jim learns that Ben once served on Flint's crew and thus knows all the current mutineers. Ben was left behind on the island after a failed treasure hunt three years ago. Jim learns that Flint buried his treasure and killed the six men who helped him bury it. Ben also mentions that he made a boat, which he hides under a white rock. He assures Jim that he can locate the treasure in return for safe passage home, and guides Jim to his dwelling. On the way there, Jim is startled to see the Union Jack, the gentleman sailor's flag, proudly waving in the distant woods.

ANALYSIS: CHAPTERS XIII–XV
The allure of the island begins to fade when the ship lands in Chapter XIII. We no longer see the island as a fantasy place and instead start to feel its dismal reality. Stevenson's descriptive language emphasizes the island's starkness and ominous aura. He makes it clear that the island is far from a tropical paradise—it is covered with "grey-coloured woods" and "naked rock." The trees appear "melancholy," and even the birds seem to be "crying all around." The foliage has a "poisonous brightness," and indeed the place may literally be poisonous: Livesey is certain that the air, which has a stagnant smell of rotting wood, will breed fever and illness. In short, Jim seems justified in his remark that "from that first look onward, I hated the very thought of Treasure Island." That he hates the "thought" of the island rather than the "sight" of it reminds us of the degree to which the characters in the novel are driven by mental interpretations of reality rather than by hard facts. Jim's perception of the island as repulsive may not be objective; rather, he may be responding solely to his mental image of the place.

Jim's sense of autonomy and free will continues to develop in these chapters, as we see his increasing ability to deal with the consequences of the mistakes he makes. When he perceives that he is not needed on board the ship, he decides on a whim to go ashore with the pirate brigade. His word choice emphasizes the casual and unreflective way he makes this decision: "It occurred to me at once to go ashore." Indeed, Jim quickly learns that perhaps he should have deliberated his decision a bit more carefully. Silver catches sight of Jim hiding in the boat, leading Jim to admit that "from that moment I began to regret what I had done." However, he is able to learn from his mistake and accept its consequences. Hiding in the forest, Jim reflects that "since I had been so foolhardy as to come ashore with these desperadoes, the least I could do was to overhear them at their councils." In this sense, he is able to make the best of his difficult situation. Jim is learning to make good use not only of his successes, but also of his errors.

Jim's concept of death begins to change in these chapters. The deaths Jim experiences earlier in the novel occur in natural or accidental fashion: Jim's father and Billy die of natural causes, and the blind beggar Pew dies in a road accident. Now the possibility of unnatural death, or murder, arises. Silver's cruel execution of Tom is the most obvious example, and it forces Jim to become aware for the first time of the possibility that one man might wish another dead. Indeed, Jim displays new awareness that he might be killed himself: he realizes he could be knifed outright like Tom or abandoned to "death by starvation" by the mutineers. It is significant that Jim believes that the island could not sustain him: in his mind, it is not a nurturing place but a place that kills. Even Ben's survival on the island is a mixed blessing: he is half mad, as if his human reason has already been killed. Indeed, from the perspective of normal human society, Ben may as well be dead, as his derangement renders him unable to conform to law or reason. In this sense, death is all around Jim—both literal death, in the form of corpses, and symbolic death, in the form of alienation from civilized society.

CHAPTERS XVI–XXI

SUMMARY: CHAPTER XVI

Dr. Livesey takes over the narration at this point, beginning his story at the mutineers' departure for the island. Discovering that Jim is with the mutineers, Livesey and Captain Smollett fear for Jim's safety, and agree that Livesey should go ashore along with Hunter, Squire Trelawney's servant. Once ashore, Livesey comes upon a stockade Flint's men built years earlier, near a spring.

Returning to the ship, Livesey tells the others what he has found. The men load two boats with provisions, taking the risk that they may arouse the suspicions of the mutineers onshore. Captain Smollett gives Abraham Gray, a sailor who has fallen in with the mutineers, a last chance to join him and his crew. Gray scuffles onto the boat, and they head for shore.

SUMMARY: CHAPTER XVII
The little boat carrying Captain Smollett, Squire Trelawney, Dr. Livesey, Tom Redruth, and Abraham Gray is dangerously overloaded and thus hard to maneuver. The men begin to suspect that the mutineers might be planning an attack, aware that the pirates possess arms and gunpowder, and that Israel Hands was once Flint's gunman. Trelawney tries to shoot Hands but hits another pirate instead, though the mutineers do not pay any attention. Hands fires a cannonball at the men's boat, causing it to founder. No lives are lost, as the water is shallow, but the men are forced to leave half of their provisions behind when they wade ashore.

SUMMARY: CHAPTER XVIII
Captain Smollett and his group make their way to the stockade and pause to reload their guns. Coming upon the pirate they have just killed, they rejoice in their success. At this instant Tom Redruth is shot. His wound is clearly fatal, and the group helps him to lie down and die nobly. Squire Trelawney kisses Tom's hand and asks for his forgiveness. All agree that he has nothing to fear in the afterworld, as he has died in the line of duty.

Trapped in the stockade, the group is bombarded by cannon fire throughout the evening. The pirates aim at the Union Jack in particular, but Smollett refuses to take in the flag. He makes an entry in his logbook of those in the stockade, while Livesey wonders what has happened to Jim. Just at this moment, Jim suddenly enters.

SUMMARY: CHAPTER XIX
Jim resumes the narration of the tale. Having seen the Union Jack flying above, he approaches the stockade along with Ben Gunn. Jim is unsure whether it is Captain Smollett's crew or the mutineers who control the stockade, but Ben, assuring him that the pirates would never fly the Union Jack, encourages him to enter. A cannon shot makes the good sailors scatter out of the stockade.

Later, Jim returns to shore to see the pirate's black flag, the Jolly
Roger, flying above the ship. The pirates' voices suggest that they
have been drinking a lot of rum. Jim enters the stockade to join
Smollett's group and tell his story. Smollett carefully assigns tasks to
the men to divide the labor, naming Jim the sentry. Smollett asks
about Ben's sanity but displays kindness to the deranged man. Jim
sleeps, but wakes to hear someone say that Long John Silver is
approaching with a flag of truce.

Summary: Chapter XX
Captain Smollett is wary of Silver's gesture of truce, fearing a trick.
The pirate announces himself as "Captain Silver," and asserts that
he wants to reach a compromise with Smollett. Smollett questions
Silver's claim to the title of captain and refuses to talk with him. Silver hoists himself over the stockade fence anyway, and approaches
Smollett. He demands the treasure map in exchange for a cease-fire.
Smollett angrily reminds Silver that he is far more powerful than the
mutineers. Silver tries again, promising the captain and his men safe
voyage in exchange for the map. When Smollett again refuses, Silver
leaves indignantly.

Summary: Chapter XXI
After roughly turning Silver away, Captain Smollett predicts that
the pirates will attack the stockade in retribution, and he orders the
men to prepare themselves. They wait in anxious expectation for an
hour, then hear a few shots and see the pirates scrambling over the
stockade fence. Gray and Squire Trelawney fire on the pirates,
wounding several of them. A fight ensues, and in the end, Smollett,
Dr. Livesey, Jim, and most of the others return safely to the stockade, having lost fewer men than the mutineers.

Analysis: Chapters XVI–XXI
Stevenson has several reasons for switching narrators from Jim to
Livesey for three chapters. The first is a practical reason: because
Jim is on shore, he is unable to narrate what is happening on board
the ship at the same time. Additionally, however, the switch in narrators gives us insight into the two characters' different perspectives. As with any first-person narrative, Jim's tale includes
subjective feelings and thoughts, and so does Livesey's. We immediately notice that there is a change in the tone of the narrative

when Livesey takes over: Livesey at times appears a bit insincere or shallow, as when he refers to the dead Tom Redruth as a "[p]oor old fellow." The most notable feature of Livesey's narrative, however, is the fact that he largely limits his narration to coverage of the events, excluding the psychological and emotional details that Jim frequently includes. Jim constantly comments about regretting an action he takes, or expresses how he hates one person or likes another. The change in narrative voice subtly reminds us that Jim's story is not simply a recounting of a series of events involving pirates and treasure, but is also a tale of his own personal and moral development.

In these chapters Stevenson continues to explore the conflict between social organization and anarchy. The half-mad Ben Gunn is an example of what happens to a man when he is removed from the protection of social structure: he loses his abilities to communicate and to be fully human. Indeed, Captain Smollett openly asks Jim whether Ben is a man, as Ben's isolation from normal society has lasted such a long time. The pirates also represent an inhuman departure from social rules and organization: as they climb over the stockade fence, Jim remarks that they resemble monkeys. Indeed, the pirates' impulsiveness and lack of forethought does lend them a somewhat animal character. The pirates have no concept of themselves as a community; while Smollett keeps a careful social register of his men and lists each of their names in his logbook, the pirates seem unconcerned with the structure or membership of their group. Additionally, whereas Smollett faithfully bids farewell to the dying Tom, the pirates pay no heed to the dead and dying among their ranks. The pirates are quick to drink rum, losing themselves in a stupor, while Smollett's men remain keen-eyed, vigilant, and capable of teamwork at all times. On the whole, while Smollett facilitates social cohesion in his group, the pirates clearly favor anarchy.

The interesting character of Long John Silver gains added depth in these chapters, especially in the scene of the attempted truce with Smollett in Chapter XXI. Here, Stevenson clearly contrasts the personalities of the two opposing leaders. Silver, in an act of brazenness, even adopts the title of captain, introducing himself as such. Though both men are resolute and persistent, insisting on their respective demands, they handle the meeting very differently. Silver heroically heaves himself over the stockade fence, climbs up the knoll, and salutes the captain in a way that Jim describes as "the handsomest style." Silver may be a mutineer, but he acts with grace and nobility. Smollett, by contrast, sits almost ridiculously in his doorway, whistling the tune "Come, Lasses and Lads," a frivolous melody arguably inappropriate to his high station. In this way, Stevenson continues to imply that while the pirates may be socially irresponsible, their inner charisma far outshines that of good men such as Smollett and Livesey.

CHAPTERS XXII–XXIV

SUMMARY: CHAPTER XXII

Seeing no further signs of attack by the mutineers, Captain Smollett and his men enjoy some leisure time in the stockade. Gray is startled to see Dr. Livesey go walking out into the trees, taking the map with him. Gray asks whether Livesey has gone mad, but Jim answers that Livesey is going to speak to Ben Gunn. Left inside to clean up the bloody mess of the earlier attack, Jim grows impatient, yearning to do something more heroic.

On another whim, Jim decides to go search for the boat that Ben had mentioned he had built. On the shore Jim glimpses Silver and his men talking and laughing, and hears the unearthly scream of Silver's parrot Cap'n Flint. After a bit of a search Jim finds the small handmade boat, which is a coracle (a type of boat once sailed by the ancient Britons). Jim decides he will sail out to the Hispaniola and cut it adrift. When darkness falls, he hoists the coracle on his shoulders and heads for the water.

SUMMARY: CHAPTER XXIII

Jim finds the coracle hard to sail, as it steers unreliably, but he eventually manages to reach the anchored ship. Grasping the hawser, or anchor rope, Jim takes out his knife and starts cutting, being careful not to let the cord snap at him when it breaks. Waiting for the wind to lessen the rope's tension so he can finish cutting it, he sits and listens to the rude oaths and drunken nonsense coming from the pirates' ship. One sailor is singing a morbid sea song about a ship setting out with a crew of seventy-five and returning with only one alive.

When there is a breeze, Jim is able to cut the last fibers of the rope and set the Hispaniola adrift. On a whim he clutches the trailing rope and hauls himself to window-level, peering in to see why no one has noticed the sudden motion of the ship. He discovers that the pirates are distracted, as Hands and another sailor are wrestling. Suddenly flung back into the coracle, Jim is startled to find that he has drifted near the pirates' campfire on shore. Sure of imminent death, he commends his soul to God and falls asleep in the coracle, dreaming of home.

SUMMARY: CHAPTER XXIV

Upon awakening, Jim discovers that he has drifted to the southwest end of Treasure Island. Paddling toward shore is useless, as he would be dashed to death on the rocks that form this edge of the island. Jim decides to try to make his way toward a friendlier shoreline to the north. After much effort he finally reaches the cove he has aimed for, his throat burning from thirst. He spots the Hispaniola drifting aimlessly and concludes that the crew either is entirely drunk or has deserted the ship.

Jim hatches a plan to try to board the wildly drifting Hispaniola, realizing that he can overtake the ship if he sits up and paddles hard. Though he runs the risk of being spotted, he thinks the idea has an air of adventure about it, so he starts paddling. Finally reaching the ship, Jim climbs on board and searches for water to quench his thirst. He hears the sound of the ship being blown into and destroying the coracle, and knows that escape from the ship is now impossible.

ANALYSIS: CHAPTERS XXII–XXIV

In these episodes Jim continues to demonstrate his tendency to follow mad whims and private impulses. Jim's restlessness and discontentment when he is cleaning up the blood from the earlier slaughter are understandable, and we sympathize with his desire to do something more grandiose and heroic. Jim does not simply dream of a heroic act, however, but actually follows through, going off to search for Ben Gunn's boat. Jim's decision to go after the boat is a wholly private one, as he does not tell anyone what he is doing. The privacy of this deed is emphasized by the fact that Jim is the only character who appears in all of Chapter XIV. In focusing so exclusively on Jim, Stevenson emphasizes the fact that *Treasure Island* is truly a coming-of-age story rather than a simple adventure tale. Though the story involves dozens of grown-up, worldly wise men, it is primarily driven—and depends upon—the solitary, private whims of a boy.

The reckless but fascinating character of the pirates also develops further in these chapters. Stevenson portrays the pirates as utterly unable to take care of their own lives in any responsible way. As Jim comes upon the Hispaniola, the ship is drifting madly from side to side, intermittently slowing and accelerating. The ship's wild course mirrors the chaotic and disorderly lives of the men who have overtaken it. The pirates cannot control or master themselves, and are unable or unwilling to guide their actions according to reason. They fail to notice the drifting of their own ship because they are busy cheering on a wrestling match, another embodiment of violence. Upon seeing the Hispaniola veering, Jim surmises that the men must all be drunk, and though he is incorrect, the pirates' rum is a clear symbol of their wayward existence. Interestingly, the pirates appear at least partly aware of their own self-destructiveness and the potentially fatal consequences of their mad lives. When they sing, their songs are about dead men's chests and ships that lose their entire crews; in a way, they sing of their own ruin. It is almost as if the pirates are obeying a sort of innate instinct toward gradual self-destruction.

Stevenson casts the tale in a new light when Jim faces death in Chapter XIII, inviting us to consider the spiritual dimension of the adventure. When Jim suddenly finds himself in close proximity to the pirates' campfire, he lies down in his boat and "devoutly recommend[s] [his] spirit to its Maker." Though Jim has clearly been aware of death before, this is the first time he shows any overt signs of religious awareness, and the first time he prays during the novel. When Jim awakens safely in the following chapter, it is as if his prayers have been answered. Alternatively, Stevenson may mean to imply that God helps those who help themselves. Jim reasons with himself to prevent the onset of panic, and is quick to use his wits and courage to paddle his boat up to the ship and hoist himself on board. Just as he gains self-awareness, courage, and maturity as he develops throughout the novel, Jim appears to be gain awareness of a higher spiritual realm as well.

CHAPTERS XXV–XXVII

SUMMARY: CHAPTER XXV

Climbing aboard the Hispaniola, Jim is surprised to see no one on deck. A bit later, however, he finds two watchmen—one is Israel Hands, who lies splashed with blood in a drunken stupor; the other is dead. Jim addresses Hands, who begs for a little brandy. Descending into the cellar, Jim finds that most of the ship's store of alcohol has been consumed. He returns with a drink for Hands and asks that Hands consider him the captain, since Jim has taken possession of the ship. In a symbolic gesture, Jim throws the pirates' flag, the Jolly Roger, overboard.

Hands offhandedly refers to the corpse next to him, insulting the dead man's Irish nationality and noting that the dead man is unable to help navigate. Hands then asserts his own navigational expertise and strikes a deal with Jim: if Jim gives Hands food, drink, and medical help, Hands will assist Jim in sailing the ship. They steer the ship toward the North Inlet of the island, enjoying a favorable wind. Jim is delighted with his new position of command, though wary of Hands's careful watch over him.

SUMMARY: CHAPTER XXVI

Jim and Hands approach the North Inlet but must wait for a favorable tide to cast anchor. Hands proposes throwing the Irishman's dead body overboard, as he objects to the corpse's presence on deck. Jim replies that he does not like the idea, and Hands responds that a dead man is simply dead. Jim retorts that the spirit never dies. Suspiciously, Hands claims that the brandy is too strong for his head and asks Jim for wine instead. Jim feigns innocence and goes to fetch some port wine, but watches Hands in secret and observes him extract a long knife from a hiding place and place it under his jacket.

Jim knows that he needs Hands to guide the ship safely into the inlet and remains wary of him. As he becomes absorbed by the effort of maneuvering the ship into its anchorage, he relaxes his vigilance and Hands attacks him. They engage in a fierce scuffle. Jim climbs up a mast and Hands follows. Jim pulls his pistol on Hands, who flings his knife, piercing Jim's shoulder and pinning him to the mast. Jim's gun goes off and Hands falls into the water.

SUMMARY: CHAPTER XXVII

*Gradually my mind came back again, my pulses
quieted down to a more natural time, and I was once
more in possession of myself.*

(See QUOTATIONS, p. 50)

The knife still pinning him against the mast, Jim watches as Hands's body rises once in the water and then sinks down. Covered in blood but not seriously wounded, Jim initially feels faint and terrified but manages to regain his composure. Shuddering, he frees himself by ripping the bit of shoulder skin that the knife has pinned to the mast. He climbs down the mast to care for his wound and, seeing the dead Irishman on deck, pushes him overboard and watches the body in the water.

Now alone on the ship, Jim decides that he is close enough to the island to swim to shore safely. He reaches the island and treks through the woods in search of Captain Smollett's stockade on the other side of the island. He finally glimpses the glow of a fire in the distance, and finds that it is coming from campfires in the stockade. Jim is surprised that Smollett would allow such a waste of firewood. Creeping into the stockade, Jim finds the men asleep. A voice suddenly cries out, "Pieces of eight!" and Jim recognizes the voice of Silver's parrot, Cap'n Flint. Realizing that the pirates have taken over the stockade, Jim tries to flee but is held tight.

ANALYSIS: CHAPTERS XXV–XXVII

Jim's authority continues to grow in these chapters. His taking control of the ship in Chapter XXV and declaration to Israel Hands that he should be addressed as captain demonstrate Jim's meteoric rise in prestige. He has promoted himself from cabin boy to captain on one single voyage. This quick ascent to power is as central to Jim's adventure as the search for treasure, and is perhaps more important; Jim, unlike the adults, devotes hardly any thought to the treasure itself or the life of leisure it can buy. As Jim stumbles into stockade and hears the parrot scream "[p]ieces of eight," we recall that the gold coins are the mutineers'—as well as Squire Trelawney's—highest goal. These "[p]ieces of eight" are not the catchphrase of Jim's own quest, however, as he is less interested in loot than in proving his worth as a hero and a man.

Jim and Hands's struggle on deck is more than a match between the good and the bad. Stevenson also gives the fight symbolic value, using it to highlight the contrast between the self-aware Jim and the self-destructive and reckless Hands. Indeed, Jim repeatedly takes firm control of his surroundings in these chapters. He tells Hands outright that he has taken possession of the ship, and later, after the fight, waits a while to climb down from the mast until, as he remarks, "I was once more in possession of myself." Hands, in sharp contrast, is unable to take possession of anything. The ship he is supposedly guarding is cut adrift and blowing about wildly while he lies on the deck drunk. Indeed, Hands's loss of control over the vessel mirrors his loss of control over himself. The symbolism of alcohol is again apparent: drunkenness, more than causing mere bodily intoxication, represents a total inability to maintain control of one's own life.

Jim's treatment of the dead Irishman's body in Chapter XXVII is unexpected, given his objection, in the preceding chapter, to Hands's suggestion that they push the corpse overboard. Jim's heaving the body into the sea without hesitation leaves us to wonder whether he had merely been pretending to care about the Irishman's eternal soul. Jim's lack of solemnity is even more jarring when contrasted with the tears Squire Trelawney sheds over Tom's dead body in Chapter XVIII. Stevenson implies that respect for the dead is a mark of proper upbringing. Granted, the Irishman is Jim's enemy, but his coldness toward the corpse is nonetheless uncharacteristic. These instances when Jim seems to straddle the line between the civilized men and the pirates make his character more interesting and complex. His sudden piratelike behavior causes us to question how conventional or complete Jim's civic and spiritual development has been.

CHAPTERS XXVIII–XXX

SUMMARY: CHAPTER XXVIII

Jim accidentally enters the pirates' camp and finds that only six of the pirates are still alive. Long John Silver addresses Jim fondly, telling the boy that he reminds Silver of what he was like when he was young. Silver tells Jim that Dr. Livesey is angry about Jim's desertion and is glad to be rid of him. Jim only partially believes this statement, but he is relieved to hear that his friends are alive. Jim realizes that Silver is having trouble managing his men, who are surly and disrespectful. Jim boldly reveals that he cut the rope on the ship and killed Hands, and he tells Silver that he does not fear him.

Silver seems merely amused by Jim, but his men threaten to become violent. Silver strives to assert his power over the mutineers, but they assemble in a far corner, leaving Silver and Jim in the other corner. Silver whispers to Jim that the men are close to another mutiny, and that he and Jim need to rely on each other to save their skins. He tells Jim to play the role of the hostage, to convince Silver's men that Silver is still in charge. Finally, Silver reveals that Livesey has given him the treasure map, which astonishes Jim.

Summary: Chapter XXIX

Jim and Silver await the end of the pirates' council. One of the pirates hands Silver a black spot, the official pirate judgment, cut out of a page of the Bible. Silver casually reads the judgment, which announces that he has been deposed from his position as a punishment for bungling the mission. Furiously, Silver retorts that if his wishes had been followed, the men would already be in possession of the treasure. He claims the failure is the fault of the men, because they forced his hand as captain. Silver also tells the men that they are all very close to being hanged. He insists on the usefulness of having Jim as hostage and reminds the men that it was he, Silver, who arranged for Dr. Livesey to tend to them every day.

As a final gesture Silver flings down the treasure map Livesey has given him, and the men gather around his side again. Silver tosses Jim the black spot as a souvenir, and Jim reads the biblical quote, from the biblical Book of Revelations, that is on the paper. Jim goes to sleep thinking of the man he has killed that day and of Silver's fate.

Summary: Chapter XXX

Jim wakes up the next morning as Dr. Livesey arrives to tend to the pirates. Jim is happy to see the doctor, but fears his disapproval. Livesey is visibly shocked to see Jim, but does not speak to him, and proceeds to treat his patients. Finally he asks to see Jim alone. One of the pirates voices a refusal, but Silver insists that that the request be granted. Jim and Livesey advance to the other side of the stockade, still in view of Silver. Livesey expresses surprise that Silver is not worried about losing his hostage, and Silver replies that he trusts Livesey as a gentleman.

Livesey accuses Jim of being cowardly in deserting the captain at a moment of weakness. Jim begins to weep. Livesey suddenly suggests that they both make a run for it and flee the pirates. Jim responds that such an action would not be right. He tells Livesey that he knows the location of the Hispaniola. Livesey exclaims that Jim manages to save their lives at every step. He returns Jim as a hostage to Silver and warns Silver not to be in any hurry to find the treasure.

ANALYSIS: CHAPTERS XXVIII–XXX

In Chapter XXX, Stevenson again addresses his recurring question of whether there is something truly noble about the pirates. Livesey, who has just chided Jim for deserting the captain in a moment of distress, suddenly encourages Jim to desert Silver. This hypocrisy contradicts Livesey's normal gentlemanly behavior and amounts to a betrayal of Silver's trust. Jim's refusal to run away is not a practical decision but an ethical one, as he says it would not be right to leave Silver at this moment. Yet even Jim's decision is highly ironic, as he willingly deserts his good captain earlier and now refuses to desert his seemingly evil enemy on moral grounds. We again wonder whether Jim secretly feels more solidarity with and respect for Long John Silver than he does for Captain Smollett. Of course, Jim is not likely to abandon society and become a lawless pirate. Nonetheless, he shares a strong spiritual sympathy with Silver, which does have good consequences. At this moment, at least, Jim comes across as more of a true gentleman than Livesey, the wealthy man of high society whose ethics we normally wouldn't question.

The pirates' inability to take care of themselves becomes even more obvious in these chapters, though the buccaneers remain fascinating and enthralling in many ways. Only six pirates remain alive, while hardly any of Smollett's men have been lost. The pirates' recklessness and lack of foresight—they burn all the firewood in one night and drink too much day after day—is at least partly to blame for their heavy losses. Even more important, the pirates continue to be dysfunctional as a group or community. Silver has difficulty managing his men and is perilously close to facing a mutiny when Jim stumbles upon him. Silver's agitated attempt to defend his own course of action suggests for the first time that he is losing his cool. When the mutineers lay out their reasons for wanting to depose Silver, Silver argues against these points out of order, suggesting his extreme anxiety. The tension within the pirates' band suggests that the group is very close to self-destruction as a social unit.

The spiritual aspect of the novel resurfaces in a small plot detail that acquires considerable symbolic importance: the black spot the pirates deliver to Silver is written on a page torn from the Book of Revelations in the Bible. The pirates seem aware that their transgression—tearing a page of the Bible—is a seriously bad omen; later, when they use the Bible to swear an oath, they wonder whether the book maintains its holiness with a page missing. The fact that the pirates dispute the Bible at a moment of crisis suggests that even the bad men cannot escape the power of the Bible's good word. Jim also seems affected by the verse inscribed on the scrap of paper, reading, "Without are dogs and murderers," an allusion to the final divine verdict that the Bible says will fall on Judgment Day. Jim falls asleep thinking about Silver's fate, as if he is close to passing judgment himself on Silver.

Chapters XXXI–XXXIV

Summary: Chapter XXXI

Silver thanks Jim for saving his life and for not running away when Dr. Livesey encouraged him to do so. Jim and Silver sit down to breakfast, and Jim is astonished by the fact that the band has prepared three times as much food as is needed. Silver's men are happy, confident of seizing the treasure soon, but Jim is sad in his certainty that Silver will betray him at the soonest practical moment.

After breakfast the pirates set off on the treasure hunt, with Silver leading Jim on a leash. They trudge through the hills, periodically pausing to consult the map. Reaching the top of a hill, the pirates are shocked to find a skeleton in seaman's garb, stretched out on the ground like a compass, pointing to the treasure. The man's knife is missing, suggesting that the pirates are not the first to have come across the skeleton. The pirates recognize the skeleton as a former mate, Allardyce, who served on Flint's crew, because of its long bones and yellow hair. Following Allardyce's clue, they head on toward the treasure.

SUMMARY: CHAPTER XXXII

Taking a rest from the search, Silver expresses his confidence that they are close to the treasure. One of the pirates feels uneasy thinking about Flint, and Silver says they are lucky the old captain is dead. The pirates suddenly hear a trembling, high voice singing the same song the pirates frequently sing, "Fifteen men on the dead man's chest." One of the pirates claims the voice is Flint's, and the men grow terrified, thinking they have awakened a ghost.

The pirates hear the voice again, and it wails what all the men recognize as Flint's last words. One of the men takes out his Bible and starts praying. Silver, the only one who remains undaunted, scorns the other men's belief in spirits and keeps focused on the search for the treasure. The pirates continue onward. As they approach the treasure site, Silver's nostrils quiver and he seems half mad. Suddenly coming upon the site, the pirates are shocked to find it has already been excavated, and only an empty hole lies before them.

SUMMARY: CHAPTER XXXIII

Silver and his men are astonished that the treasure is gone. Silver hands Jim his gun, realizing that he needs the boy after all. Jim coldly accuses Silver of changing sides again. The men dig in the pit and find a few coins. One of them accuses Silver of having known all along that the treasure was gone. The angered pirates suddenly seem united against Silver and begin to move upon him. Suddenly a gun fires from somewhere in the surrounding thicket, cutting down several of the pirates. Silver draws his pistol, killing the pirate who had accused him. Dr. Livesey, Ben Gunn, and Abraham Gray emerge from the trees, their muskets smoking.

Silver thanks Livesey for saving him from the uprising and greets Ben Gunn affectionately. We learn that Ben, in his wanderings about the island, had come across the skeleton, dug up the treasure, and moved it to a cave. Livesey found out about Ben's actions and gave the map to Silver only after he knew it was useless. Learning that Jim would be among the disappointed treasure-seekers, Livesey sent Ben off to imitate Captain Flint's voice, playing on the pirates' superstitions and slowing their progress.

Finally, the group goes to the cave and finds the vast treasure of gold just where Ben left it. Captain Smollett tells Jim that he will never go to sea with him again. They all enjoy a good meal together, with Jim especially happy among his friends.

SUMMARY: CHAPTER XXXIV

> *[T]he worst dreams that ever I have are when I*
> *hear . . . the sharp voice of Captain Flint still ringing*
> *in my ears: "Pieces of eight! pieces of eight!"*
> (See QUOTATIONS, p. 51)

The next morning, the men begin the difficult task of transporting all the gold down to the Hispaniola. Jim is fascinated by the coins— far more by the variety of their designs and nations of origin than by the wealth they represent. On the evening of the third day of loading the ship, the men discover three of the mutineers, who are either drunk or crazy. The men decide to leave the three mutineers marooned on the island with a small amount of provisions.

As Captain Smollett and his men finally make preparations to embark, the three mutineers kneel before them in submission, begging to be taken on board. Understanding that they are being left behind, they fire at the departing ship, but no one is hurt. Smollett sets course for a port in Spanish America before turning home. The Hispaniola eventually returns to Bristol.

Stepping back from his tale, Jim reports that Captain Smollett is retired from the sea life, that Ben has spent his reward and is now a lodge-keeper, and that Silver crept overboard one night during the voyage with a few bags of the treasure, never to be heard from again. Jim wishes Silver well. He notes that the remainder of the treasure still lies buried on the island, but claims that nothing would ever induce him to take part in another treasure hunt. He says that he still has nightmares of Silver's parrot crying, "Pieces of eight! pieces of eight!"

ANALYSIS: CHAPTERS XXXI–XXXIV

Spirituality and the treasure come together in these last chapters, as the searching pirates are guided by a dead man and imagine themselves pursued by spirits. Approaching the treasure means approaching death, spirits, and even the Bible, which one of the pirates reads frantically in an attempt to appease the spirits that he believes are haunting them. Though the spirits are merely a trick devised by Livesey, Stevenson nonetheless wants us to make a serious connection between the treasure hunt and spirituality. Stevenson has a skeleton literally point the way to the treasure, reiterating the spiritual significance of the treasure hunt. Likewise, he questions the value of money that one sacrifices one's integrity trying to find. Stevenson suggests that a man's greed can cause him to lose part of his humanity. Just as the skeleton is literally a destroyed human, the greedy pirates are doomed to self-destruction. Ironically, the treasure is not even there anymore; the pirates are pursuing fool's gold, while the real bounty lies hidden elsewhere, waiting for the good men to uncover it.

Additionally, Stevenson questions the actual value of the treasure. Though the treasure is the very thing that prompts the whole adventure, and which gives the island and the novel their names, Jim hardly mentions it at the end. We assume that Jim wins his hard-earned share of the loot, but we are never absolutely certain, because he does not refer to it at all. Indeed, the treasure itself seems insignificant to Jim. Even when the group first finds it hidden away in Ben's cave, Jim does not think about the pleasure and leisure it can buy, but rather of the "blood and sorrow" it has cost. The treasure is literally a heavy burden to bear when Jim and the men carry it down to the Hispaniola. Later, though Jim is fascinated by the national origins of the coins and their designs, he is uninterested in their financial power or value. Ironically, then, the final lesson of *Treasure Island* for Jim may be that treasure is not such a prize after all.

In the final passage of the novel, Stevenson again makes us wonder whom Jim cares about most in this novel. In the concluding paragraphs, Jim mentions only Captain Smollett, Ben Gunn, Abraham Gray, and Long John Silver, men whom he meets after his voyage has started. He does not talk about Dr. Livesey and Squire Trelawney, the men with whom he starts the voyage. Though Livesey and Trelawney represent the heights of science and aristocracy, the fruits of civilization, Jim does not think about either of them at the end of his tale, and we sense that they do not matter to him anymore. Considering the bloodshed Silver has caused, in contrast to the assistance Livesey has provided, it seems disrespectful for Jim to wish the pirate well while ignoring the doctor. Nonetheless, Livesey and Trelawney do not inspire Jim in the way that Silver has. Jim certainly has not been recruited into piracy, but Silver and his pirates have influenced him all the same. We are certain that Jim will not grow up to become like either Livesey or Trelawney; rather, he will be a mix of reason and rationality, spirit and charisma.

Important Quotations Explained

1. Fifteen men on the dead man's chest—
   Yo-ho-ho, and a bottle of rum!
   Drink and the devil had done for the rest—
   Yo-ho-ho, and a bottle of rum!

This pirate's ditty, first sung in Chapter I and recalled many times afterward, remains one of the best-known legacies of *Treasure Island*. The poem encapsulates drink, death, and wickedness, which are inextricably linked to the pirates, and which give them an aura of wild glamour. The "bottle of rum" recalls the almost constant state of drunkenness of Silver's ragged brigade. This reference to alcohol is also connected to idea of the "dead man," as the pirates' drunkenness results in mishaps, losses, and deaths, and is perhaps responsible for their ultimate failure.

The "dead man's chest" symbolically refers to both Billy Bones's sea chest and Flint's hidden treasure. The pirates' song associates the treasure chest with a dead man rather than a living one, suggesting that the pirates are unconsciously aware that their mission will end in death and failure. In a sense, they are singing of their own downfall, almost displaying a death drive. The image of the dead man's chest also refers to the way in which greed leads to a man's loss of soul and also recalls the ultimate futility of finding material treasure, as all humans eventually die in the end.

2. "I have only one thing to say to you, sir … if you keep on drinking rum, the world will soon be quit of a very dirty scoundrel!"

These words, which Dr. Livesey addresses to Billy Bones in Chapter I, emphasize the conflict between the civilized world and the lawless criminal world in *Treasure Island*. Billy has usurped power for himself, as he refuses to pay his bills and assumes that everyone will immediately fall silent whenever he slaps the dining-room table. Billy's power is, in fact, quite real: Jim's innkeeper father is too scared of Billy to demand payment, and everyone does stop talking when the seaman slaps the table. Though Billy is a stranger in the area, shows no special virtues, and has no political or financial power, he nonetheless holds an extraordinary and mysterious power over everyone. This power, which Long John Silver also displays, fascinates Jim. Power of this sort is an insult to the civilized world, as it offends the values of order, responsibility, and propriety. The practical Dr. Livesey, who embodies the traditional, ordered world, predicts that the rum will soon kill Billy and declares that the pirates are scoundrels. Livesey judges the pirates through the lens of his own world and its accompanying values. However, by the end of the novel, we learn that both the doctor's world and the pirates' world are flawed, and that both worlds can inspire and destroy.

3. "Well, squire ... I don't put much faith in your
    discoveries, as a general thing; but I will say this, John
    Silver suits me."

Dr. Livesey delivers these remarks to Squire Trelawney at the end of
Chapter VIII, when the men first meet the crew that will accompany
them to Treasure Island. This quotation raises the issue of judgment
of another person's character. First, Livesey's skepticism about
Trelawney's prudence suggests that the squire's knowledge of
human affairs might be less reliable than that of the practical man of
science. We later verify this hypothesis when we discover that the
squire has been tricked into manning his ship with a band of pirates;
his judgment is indeed unsound. Yet Long John Silver tricks even the
wise Dr. Livesey. Though in reality the ringleader of the pirates, Silver is a man whom Livesey trusts instinctively. The doctor's trust
suggests that Silver has extraordinary powers of deception, but also
that there is something genuinely likable about the pirate. Even
though Silver is a miscreant, he is charismatic and repeatedly earns
the respect of others. Indeed, Silver wins Jim's affection and admira-
tion by the end of the adventure, and he acts like a gentleman on several occasions. Livesey and Trelawney are deceived by Silver
because he is such a contradictory character, not fully good but not
fully evil either.

4. I was no sooner certain of this than I began to feel
    sick, faint, and terrified. The hot blood was running
    over my back and chest. The dirk, where it had pinned
    my shoulder to the mast, seemed to burn like a hot
    iron; yet it was not so much these real sufferings that
    distressed me ... it was the horror I had upon my mind
    of falling from the cross-trees into that still green
    water beside the body of the coxswain. I clung with
    both hands till my nails ached, and I shut my eyes as if
    to cover up the peril. Gradually my mind came back
    again, my pulses quieted down to a more natural time,
    and I was once more in possession of myself.

Jim has these thoughts at the beginning of Chapter XXVII, when he realizes that he has killed Israel Hands, the pirate who has wounded Jim with his dagger. This passage reveals Jim's maturity and his developing sense of self. The pirates are always drunken, rowdy, and impetuous, and demonstrate little or no ability to manage the situations or circumstances that surround them. Jim, conversely, almost immediately after the fight is over, Jim shows his developing ability to emerge from a state of passionate agitation to a state of control. Jim takes possession of himself in a mature and responsible fashion, and then takes control of the ship and names himself captain. The difference between Jim and Israel Hands represents the difference between those who can take care of themselves and those who cannot. Israel is still drunk when he dies, while Jim is in full possession of his mind and senses.

The passage also shows the importance of Jim's newfound sense of personal identity. The physical suffering Jim experiences is not as troubling as the prospect of being next to Israel Hands in the water. Jim cannot bear the thought of being associated with a pirate, a person who is not in control of his own body and mind. Jim clearly defines himself as separate from a pirate or criminal—he identifies himself as an honest young man. Jim's identity matters more to him than even physical pain, suggesting that he is developing a sense of identity, confidence, and maturity.

5. The bar silver and the arms still lie, for all that I know,
where Flint buried them; and certainly they shall lie
there for me. Oxen and wain-ropes would not bring
me back again to that accursed island; and the worst
dreams that ever I have are when I hear the surf
booming about its coasts, or start upright in bed, with
the sharp voice of Captain Flint still ringing in my
ears: 'Pieces of eight! pieces of eight!'

These final lines of the novel summarize Jim's feelings about his
adventure. Ironically, one of the results of Jim's treasure hunt is that
he learns he does not actually want the treasure, and that he is happy
to leave the silver buried on the island. Similarly, at the end of the
novel, Jim also realizes that he does not truly want adventure. The
negative tone with which he closes his account seems out of place, as
in the end everything has worked out well for him: Jim is safely back
home, his friends have survived, and he presumably possesses a fair
share of the pirates' loot as reward. Yet Jim calls the island
"accursed," and he is plagued by nightmares of treasure and Silver's
screeching parrot.

Jim's continuing dreams signify that his adventure is still with
him, for better or for worse, and that his experience with the pirates
has had an indelible impact on his life. However, it also appears that
the tragedies of the adventure—the greed and death—still trouble
him. Though Captain Flint is long dead and buried, and Jim is back
in the relative safety of the civilized world, he still feels the influence
and temptation of the pirates' underworld. Jim is having trouble
adjusting to the upright, civilized world and the fact that it completely rejects the darker, more lawless world of the pirates. That a
pirate literally has the last words in the novel (the parrot's cry of
"pieces of eight!") shows that the pirates, and the life and values
they represent, will always haunt Jim and the civilized world.

QUOTATIONS

KEY FACTS

FULL TITLE
Treasure Island

AUTHOR
Robert Louis Stevenson

TYPE OF WORK
Novel

GENRE
Children's book, adventure story, coming-of-age story

LANGUAGE
English

TIME AND PLACE WRITTEN
1881, Scotland

DATE OF FIRST PUBLICATION
1883

PUBLISHER
Cassell and Company

NARRATOR
Jim Hawkins is both the hero of the tale and the narrator for all but three chapters—Dr. Livesey narrates Chapters XV–XVIII. Jim narrates the tale because Dr. Livesey and Squire Trelawney ask him to recount the events after the end of the adventure.

POINT OF VIEW
Jim narrates from first-and third-person perspectives. In doing so, he presents plot developments that only he himself observes. Livesey does the same in his portion of the narrative. Whereas Jim describes his state of mind, feelings, and attitudes throughout his tale, Livesey is more objectively factual in his narration.

TONE

Jim's attitudes toward his life and his adventure are significant. The fact that he hardly mentions his parents, even after his father's death, suggests indifference toward his family. Jim shows moderate respect, and occasional impatience, when describing Captain Smollett and Dr. Livesey. When Jim describes the pirates, his tone suggests that he admires and reveres them, and is certainly fascinated by them. Jim's tone is generally modest when narrating his own heroic feats.

TENSE

Past

SETTING (TIME)

During the eighteenth century

SETTING (PLACE)

Near Bristol, England, and Treasure Island, an island off the coast of "Spanish America"

PROTAGONIST

Jim Hawkins

MAJOR CONFLICT

Jim, Squire Trelawney, Dr. Livesey, Captain Smollett, and his crew search for a treasure that Captain Flint, an old pirate, has left buried after his death. They are challenged by Flint's former crewmembers, who have tricked Trelawney into hiring them to help sail to Treasure Island.

RISING ACTION

The discovery of the treasure map in the inn; the hiring of a treacherous crew for the expedition; the voyage to Treasure Island; the mutiny of Silver and his crew; Silver taking Jim as a hostage

CLIMAX

The pirates' and Jim's discovery that the treasure has already been excavated from its burial ground

FALLING ACTION

The return trip to England; Silver's escape with some of the treasure; Jim's nightmares about the sea and gold coins

THEMES

The search for heroic role models; the futility of desire; the lack of adventure in the modern age; the hunger for adventure; the vanity of pursuing wealth; the process of growing up and proving oneself

MOTIFS

Solitude; animals; the color black; singing; physical handicaps; betrayal

SYMBOLS

The coracle; the treasure map; rum; the black spot; Ben Gunn's insanity; the skeleton pointing the way to the treasure; the empty treasure site

FORESHADOWING

Billy Bones is handed his black spot and dies soon thereafter; Captain Smollett is suspicious of his new crew, which turns out to be mutinous; Mr. Arrow repeatedly gets drunk, then disappears from the ship; Jim sees Israel Hands hide a knife under his jacket, and Hands soon attacks him; the sailors sing about a dead man's chest before the adventure has begun, and almost all of them end up dead in the end

KEY FACTS

STUDY QUESTIONS & ESSAY TOPICS

STUDY QUESTIONS

1. *Why do you think Stevenson chooses a boy to narrate this tale?*

In the very first sentence of the novel, Jim tells us that he is recounting the story of Treasure Island because Squire Trelawney, Dr. Livesey, and other gentlemen have asked him to write it down. Stevenson's choice of Jim as a narrator is noteworthy and unexpected, since the adult men have greater life experience, education, and verbal skills than this young boy has, and would seem to be able to bring more perspective to the narrative.

Nonetheless, Stevenson chooses Jim as the storyteller in order to give us a personal, subjective account of the adventure, which is just as important as the objective plot events that take place. A large part of Jim's adventure is his development from a sheltered, protected young boy into a responsible, freethinking, charismatic young man. We would not be as emotionally invested in the treasure hunt, or feel as conflicted about the two sides—the pirate world and the civilized world—if Jim were not the narrator. The novel would not have the same tensions, passions, and suspense if Livesey narrated the tale. Jim's coming-of-age from childhood to adulthood would likely not figure in the novel at all if it were told by another character or an external narrator. The novel's subjective elements—such as Jim's admission that he had to struggle to regain his composure after the fight with Israel, or his regret at the decision to go ashore with the pirates—might be lost in the hands of another narrator. Instead, with Jim narrating, we see that he is learning about himself and developing his own moral character. Without this subjective side, the novel would just be a narration of events, rather than a more complex history of a boy becoming a man, the process of forming his identity, and an exploration of what comprises a human being.

2.   *Discuss the role of Ben Gunn in the novel. Why does
     Stevenson include this character, and why does he describe
     Ben as he does?*

Ben Gunn is one of the novel's strangest characters. He does not
receive much attention in the narrative, yet his inclusion in the novel
is crucial. Ben Gunn saves Jim at the end, and he is the one who has
first discovered the treasure—notably, without the aid of the treasure map. Ben should be a hero, but in his deranged and ragged state
everyone thinks of him as pathetic, merely a skeleton of a man,
despite all his heroic accomplishments. Ben has long been separated
from the rules and rationality of society, and the fact that he has
moved away from following social norms causes others to view him
as insane. Fittingly, Ben saves Jim by spookily imitating dead
pirates, as he himself is something of a ghost of a man. Ben has
attained riches and fortune, but he has lost his reason and his
humanity in the process. He is a cautionary example of a man who
has lost everything because of his pirate lifestyle and greedy mental-
ity. Ben's avarice, selfishness, and desire have brought him only the
status of a castaway—a literal outcast of society.

3. *Why does Stevenson make such an effort to show Long John Silver's positive traits?*

Many who have heard of Long John Silver assume that he is the indisputable villain of *Treasure Island* and are surprised upon reading the novel that he actually has a number of positive character traits. Silver is much more than the stereotyped villain of a melodrama: he is a complex and vital character who, like any character of great depth, displays virtues as well as moral flaws. Certainly he is a thief, a cold-hearted killer, and a devious manipulator with no sense of loyalty, but to dismiss him as only these things would be too hasty.

Silver also displays admirable characteristics that inspire and influence Jim. Jim imitates Silver's capacity for spontaneous, independent thought and action, following his own whims on several occasions and even deserting his own crew. Jim also develops Silver's strength and agility, as he demonstrates when he pulls himself up onto the ship from his foundering boat. At times, Jim even seems fond of Silver, and wishes him well at the end of the novel. Indeed, Silver tells Jim that he reminds him of himself as a young boy, an explicit indicator of the similarity between the two characters. *Treasure Island* is such a rich adventure story in part because Stevenson allows its hero to resemble its ostensible villain. Many of Jim's heroic actions are inspired, at least in part, by the villainous Silver's spirit. Stevenson implies that the line between right and wrong, good and evil, is often quite ambiguous.

SUGGESTED ESSAY TOPICS

1. Compare Captain Smollett's leadership abilities to those of Long John Silver. The two men lead their crews in very different ways. What do their individual styles reveal about the two characters?

2. Jim never refers to the island as anything other than Treasure Island, but Treasure Island is only the voyagers' private nickname for the place. Why doesn't Jim or Stevenson reveal a more geographically accurate name for this island? Does this name change our perception of the place?

3. The only examples of religious activity in this novel occur toward the end. Why do you think Stevenson shows his characters' religious side only near the end of their adventure?

4. Though there is nothing political or colonial about Squire Trelawney's expedition, flags appear frequently in this novel. Since Treasure Island is not being claimed as a British territory, the function of the flags seems more symbolic than political. Why are flags so important in *Treasure Island*?

5. On Treasure Island, Jim earns the respect of his colleagues and successfully discovers the fortune he sought. In light of these successes, why does Jim nonetheless have an aversion to Treasure Island?

REVIEW & RESOURCES

QUIZ

1. What does Jim's father do for a living?

   A. He is a farmer
   B. He is a banker
   C. He is an innkeeper
   D. He is a lawyer

2. Why does Billy give Jim money each month?

   A. To shine his boots
   B. To bring him rum
   C. To be on the lookout for Billy's enemy
   D. To guard his map

3. Where is Billy when he receives the black spot?

   A. On the road
   B. In the inn
   C. On the ship
   D. At the squire's house

4. In what century is *Treasure Island* set?

   A. Seventeenth
   B. Eighteenth
   C. Nineteenth
   D. Twentieth

5. What is Pew's most noticeable physical feature?

   A. His blindness
   B. His lameness
   C. His leprosy
   D. His deafness

6. To whom does Jim first show the map?

    A. Pew
    B. His father
    C. Captain Smollett
    D. Dr. Livesey

7. What is Long John Silver's original job on the ship?

    A. Captain
    B. Cook
    C. First mate
    D. Doctor

8. Where is Jim when he overhears Silver's plans for mutiny?

    A. In the wine cellar
    B. In an apple barrel
    C. In the washroom
    D. In the stockade

9. Where does Jim encounter Ben Gunn?

    A. On the ship
    B. In the stockade
    C. At the pirates' camp
    D. In the woods

10. What does Jim hunt for after leaving Captain Smollett in the stockade?

    A. Treasure
    B. Rum
    C. Medicine
    D. A boat

11. How does Jim move the ship away from the pirate camp?

    A. He cuts it adrift
    B. He sails it at night
    C. He bribes the crew
    D. He pulls it with his boat

12. What is the name of Long John Silver's parrot?

    A. Cap'n Flint
    B. Cap'n Hook
    C. Cap'n Billy
    D. Cap'n Morgan

13. Who is the first to discover Flint's treasure on the island?

    A. Silver
    B. Jim
    C. Ben Gunn
    D. Livesey

14. How does Ben Gunn frighten the pirates?

    A. By putting spiders in their beds
    B. By imitating the dead Flint's voice
    C. By telling them their rum supply has run out
    D. By telling them the treasure map is a hoax

15. Who interrupts Jim's narration to tell the story for a while?

    A. Smollett
    B. Silver
    C. Trelawney
    D. Livesey

16. Whom does Jim fight on the ship when he sneaks on board?

    A. Israel Hands
    B. Tom Redruth
    C. Long John Silver
    D. Arrow

17. When the treasure was initially discovered, where was it taken immediately after its excavation?

    A. To the ship
    B. To the stockade
    C. To a cave
    D. To the river

18. Why does Silver visit Smollett in the stockade?

A. To make a truce
B. To extort money
C. To take a hostage
D. To fetch medicine

19. When the pirates hand Silver a black spot toward the end of the novel, what is its message?

A. That Silver has one day to find the treasure
B. That Silver has been deposed
C. That Silver will be executed
D. That Silver will be marooned

20. Which of the following characters does Silver take hostage?

A. Ben
B. Smollett
C. Livesey
D. Jim

21. How does Billy Bones die?

A. Silver kills him
B. From a stroke
C. From gangrene
D. He is hanged for piracy

22. What does Hispaniola signify in the novel?

A. The name of the island
B. The name of Silver's wife
C. The name of the ship
D. The name of the inn

23. What is the last clue guiding the pirates to the treasure site?

A. A skeleton
B. A mark on a tree
C. An overturned chest
D. An unfurled flag

24. What happens to Silver at the end of the novel?

    A. He is hanged
    B. He is marooned on the island
    C. He returns to England
    D. He steals some of the treasure and sneaks away

25. What flag does Smollett fly over the stockade?

    A. The White Cross
    B. The Jolly Roger
    C. The Union Jack
    D. The Green Moon

SUGGESTIONS FOR FURTHER READING

BELL, IAN. *Dreams of Exile: Robert Louis Stevenson, a Biography.* New York: Henry Holt, 1993.

BRYAN, FRANCIS. *Jim Hawkins and the Curse of Treasure Island.* London: Orion, 2001.

CALDER, JENNI. *Robert Louis Stevenson: A Life Study.* New York: Oxford University Press, 1980.

CHESTERTON, G. K. *Robert Louis Stevenson.* New York: Sheed and Ward, 1955.

DAICHES, DAVID. *Robert Louis Stevenson and His Word.* London: Thames and Hudson, 1973.

EIGNER, EDWIN M. *Robert Louis Stevenson and Romantic Tradition.* Princeton, New Jersey: Princeton University Press, 1966.

HAMMOND, J. R. *A Robert Louis Stevenson Companion: A Guide to the Novels, Essays, and Short Stories.* New York: Macmillan, 1984.

KIELY, ROBERT. *Robert Louis Stevenson and the Fiction of Adventure.* Cambridge, Massachusetts: Harvard University Press, 1964.

REVIEW & RESOURCES

SparkNotes Study Guides: